PowerKids Readers:

Clean and Healthy!
All Day Long™

Washing My Hands

Elizabeth Vogel

The Rosen Publishing Group's
PowerKids Press™
New York

Published in 2001 by The Rosen Publishing Group, Inc.
29 East 21st Street, New York, NY 10010

Copyright © 2001 by The Rosen Publishing Group, Inc.

First Edition

Book Design: Felicity Erwin
Layout: Emily Muschinske

Photo Illustrations by Thaddeus Harden

Vogel, Elizabeth.
      Washing my hands / Elizabeth Vogel.
         p. cm.— (PowerKids Readers clean and healthy all day long)
      Includes index.
      Summary: A girl describes how she washes her hands and gives examples of times when hand washing is important.
      ISBN 0-8239-5684-9
      1. Children—Health and hygiene—Juvenile literature. 2. Hand washing—Juvenile literature. [1. Hand washing. 2. Cleanliness. 3. Health.]

RA777.V64 2000
613'.0432—dc21   00-039175

Manufactured in the United States of America

Contents

3

Vicky's mom washes her hands. Vicky's mom says that washing your hands helps you stay clean and healthy.

After Vicky sneezes, she needs to wash her hands. Dirty hands can spread germs.

You wash your hands in the sink. You need soap and water to wash your hands.

9

Vicky rubs the soap on her hands. She rubs the soap on her fingers. She rubs the soap on her palms. She rubs the soap on her wrists, too.

Vicky rinses her hands with water. The water takes the soap off.

Vicky dries her hands on the towel.

15

It is good to wash your
hands before you eat.

It is good to wash your hands after you go to the bathroom.

19

It is good to wash your hands after you finger paint, too!

Words to Know

SINK

SOAP

SNEEZE

TOWEL

WATER

Here are more books to read about washing your hands:

Washing Your Hands
by Crystal Stevens
Hubbard Scientific Co.

Body Buddies Say..."Wash Your Hands!"
by Leeann Wenkman
Sunrise Publications

To learn more about washing your hands, check out this Web site:
http://www.eatright.org/feature/060199.html

Index

Word Count: 131

Note to Librarians, Teachers, and Parents

PowerKids Readers are specially designed to get emergent and beginning readers excited about learning to read. Simple stories and concepts are paired with photographs of real kids in real-life situations. Spirited characters and story lines that kids can relate to help readers respond to written language by linking meaning with their own everyday experiences. Sentences are short and simple, employing a basic vocabulary of sight words, as well as new words that describe familiar things and places. Large type, clean design, and photographs corresponding directly to the text all help children to decipher meaning. Features such as a picture glossary and an index help children get the most out of PowerKids Readers. Lists of related books and Web sites encourage kids to explore other sources and to continue the process of learning. With their engaging stories and vivid photo-illustrations, PowerKids Readers inspire children with the interest and confidence to return to these books again and again. It is this rich and rewarding experience of success with language that gives children the opportunity to develop a love of reading and learning that they will carry with them throughout their lives.